YOU KNOW YOU'RE
A New Parent
WHEN...

By Jeff Justice & Diane Pfeifer

Illustrated by Clark Taylor

Published by Strawberry Patch, Atlanta, Georgia

ISBN: 0-9618306-5-4
Library of Congress: 91-65001
Published by: Strawberry Patch
            P.O. Box 52404
            Atlanta, Georgia 30355

Editor: Diane Pfeifer
Design & Composition: Paula Chance, Peachtree Type & Design
Photography: Pat Cahill

We dedicate this book to Jennica Snow Justice
who has blessed us with sweet smiles and sleepless nights;
and most of all, to God for blessing all new parents.
Sai Ram.

WHEN...

your video camera is
permanently attached
to your eye.

WHEN...

nobody notices YOU anymore.

WHEN...

the photo shop starts charging
you by the pound.

WHEN...

you buy a $300 baby car seat
for a $200 car.

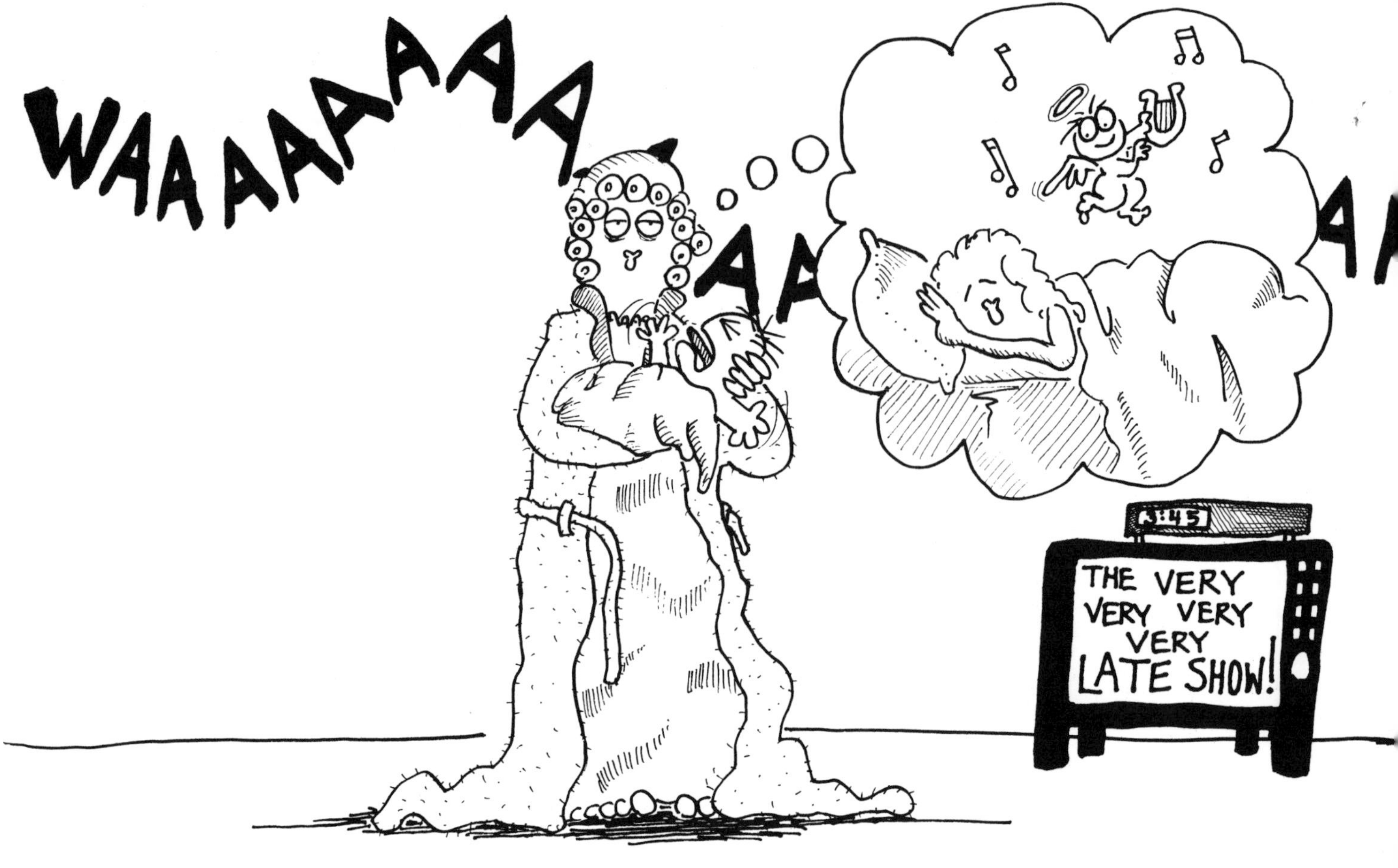
WAAAAAAAA
AA
A
3:45
THE VERY VERY VERY VERY LATE SHOW!

WHEN...

you dream of sleeping.

WHEN...

you check out babies
instead of babes.

WHEN...

you call the paramedics
at the first sniffle.

WHEN...

you could spot your car
from Jupiter.

WHEN...

the boss of the family
wears plastic pants.

WHEN...

you're more excited about
a new tooth
than a new car.

WHEN...

your baby finally sleeps through
the night—and you can't.

WHEN...

you spend more money calling
home than on the meal.

WHEN...

you think your baby
is so special
that three wise men will appear.

WHEN...

you could open
a bumper car ride
in your living room.

WHEN...

your purse becomes a
photo album.

WHEN...

you only park now
to change a diaper.

WHEN...

a "power lunch" is strained
beets and carrots.

WHEN...

you become a human pretzel
to keep the baby asleep.

WHEN...

your baby's mouth becomes
the lost and found.

WHEN...

going to work
feels like a vacation.

WHEN...

you consider yourself on time
If you arrive the same day.

WHEN...

there's more food on you than
in the baby's tummy.

WHEN...

your bathtub becomes
a marina.

WHEN...

your labor story could have been
directed by Steven Spielberg.

WHEN...

5 o'clock isn't happy hour
anymore.

WHEN...

you maintain radio contact
at all times.

WHEN...

it takes you two hours
to change
an eight-pound baby.

WHEN...

everyone you know becomes
Dr. Spock.

WHEN...

the baby wears designer originals
and you're in
red-tag specials.

WHEN...

a night on the town is driving
the baby around at 2 a.m.

WHEN...

you pack for an hour and a half
just to go to the store.

DO YOU THINK THE B-A-B-Y WILL BE ALRIGHT WITH THE S-I-T-T-E-R?
NOT ON YOUR L-I-F-E.
DADDY

WHEN...

you start spelling
e-v-e-r-y-t-h-i-n-g.

WHEN...

you think you deserve a medal
if the baby's washed and
fed by 5 p.m.

SHADDUP AND ROCK!
ROCK ALL NIGHT
SLEEPY BEAR BED TIME STORIES

WHEN...

you do all your rockin' in a chair.

WHEN...

you need an addition
on the house for stuffed animals.

WHEN...

party time becomes potty time.

WHEN...

your silk blouse becomes
a silk handkerchief.

WHEN...

romance is something
you hear about
from your single friends.

WHEN...

everyone's staring at YOU
in the store now.

WHEN...

you finally get a night out together
and spend it
thinking about the baby.

WHEN...

your briefcase becomes
inhabited by bears.

WHEN...

your house is so baby-proofed
even you can't open
the cabinets.

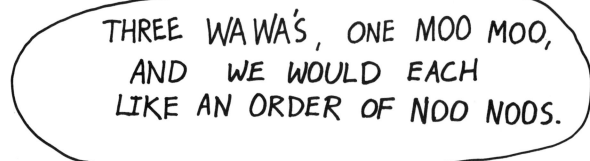

WHEN...

you find new words creeping into
your vocabulary.

WHEN...

you start ordering
your meals cold.

WHEN...

everyone asks when
you're going to have
another one.

By Jeff Justice

KNOW AN EXPECTANT COUPLE?

This hilarious spoof tackles those impossible pregnant questions
every future father faces. Perfect for showers or pregnancy announcements.
Cartoons by Clark Taylor.

To order **The Pregnant Husband's Handbook** or **You Know You're A New Parent When...**
by charge, call **1-800-875-7242** during business hours (EST) or send check or money
order for $5.95 plus $1 shipping to: **Strawberry Patch, Box 52404-Y, Atlanta, GA 30355**